Pg. 11~
Y.A

8/19

Pg. 247

12 - titles

WRESTLING BIOGRAPHIES

BRAUN STROWMAN:
MONSTER AMONG MEN

Fly!
An Imprint of Abdo Zoom
abdobooks.com

KENNY ABDO

abdobooks.com

Published by Abdo Zoom, a division of ABDO, P.O. Box 398166, Minneapolis, Minnesota 55439. Copyright © 2020 by Abdo Consulting Group, Inc. International copyrights reserved in all countries. No part of this book may be reproduced in any form without written permission from the publisher. Fly!™ is a trademark and logo of Abdo Zoom.

Printed in the United States of America, North Mankato, Minnesota.
052019
092019

THIS BOOK CONTAINS RECYCLED MATERIALS

Photo Credits: Alamy, AllWrestlingSuperstars.com, AP Images, Getty Images, Shutterstock, © Mmsnapplez p8 / CC BY-SA 4.0, © Megan Elice Meadows p9 / CC BY-SA 2.0, © Miguel Discart p13, p14, p20 / CC BY-SA 2.0, © Bryan Horowitz p18 / CC BY-SA 2.0
Production Contributors: Kenny Abdo, Jennie Forsberg, Grace Hansen
Design Contributors: Dorothy Toth, Neil Klinepier

Library of Congress Control Number: 2018963794

Publisher's Cataloging-in-Publication Data

Names: Abdo, Kenny, author.
Title: Braun Strowman: monster among men / by Kenny Abdo.
Other title: Monster among men
Description: Minneapolis, Minnesota : Abdo Zoom, 2020 | Series: Wrestling biographies set 2 | Includes online resources and index.
Identifiers: ISBN 9781532127526 (lib. bdg.) | ISBN 9781532128509 (ebook) | ISBN 9781532128998 (Read-to-me ebook)
Subjects: LCSH: Wrestlers--United States--Biography--Juvenile literature. | World Wrestling Entertainment Studios--Juvenile literature.
Classification: DDC 796.812092 [B]--dc23

TABLE OF CONTENTS

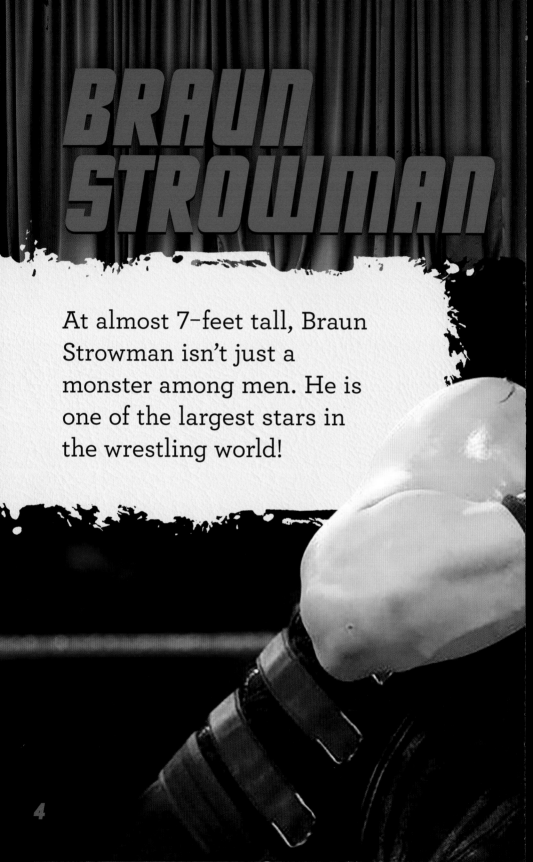

BRAUN STROWMAN

At almost 7-feet tall, Braun Strowman isn't just a monster among men. He is one of the largest stars in the wrestling world!

There is more to the WWE giant than his size. Strowman is big in personality and talent as a reigning Greatest Royal Rumble champion.

EARLY YEARS

Adam Scherr was born in Sherrills Ford, North Carolina, in 1983.

He grew nearly a foot (.3 m) and added more than 100 pounds (45.3 kg) in high school. Scherr wrestled, played football, and ran track. In 2003, he enrolled in community college. He also played football semi-professionally for the Hickory Hornets.

After college, Scherr participated in Strongman contests. He won the US Amateur National **Championship** in 2011. In 2012, he won the World Championship. Scherr was spotted by wrestler Mark Henry as WWE potential.

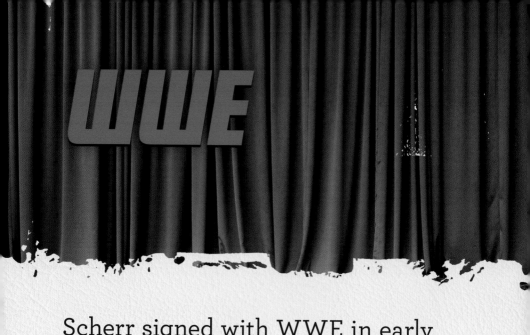

Scherr signed with WWE in early 2013 as Braun Strowman. He made his **debut** in December 2014. Strowman defeated Chad Gable in the **match**.

Strowman joined the Wyatt Family in 2015. He made his **roster debut** in a **match** against Dean Ambrose and Roman Reigns.

Strowman fought in his first pay-per-view event **match** called the Night of Champions later that year. The Wyatt Family defeated Ambrose, Reigns, and Chris Jericho in the six-man **tag team** match.

Strowman wanted to fight in the Raw Tag Team **Championship** during **WrestleMania** 34. But he didn't have a **tag team** partner.

He randomly picked a 10-year-old fan out of the stands to fight with him. Together, they won the **championship**!

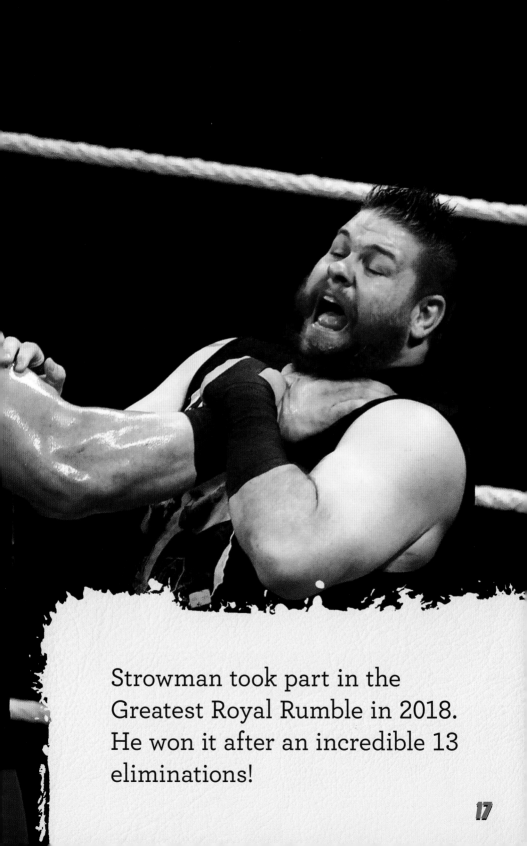

Strowman took part in the
Greatest Royal Rumble in 2018.
He won it after an incredible 13
eliminations!

Strowman holds the record for most eliminations in a single Elimination Chamber and Royal Rumble **match** in WWE history.

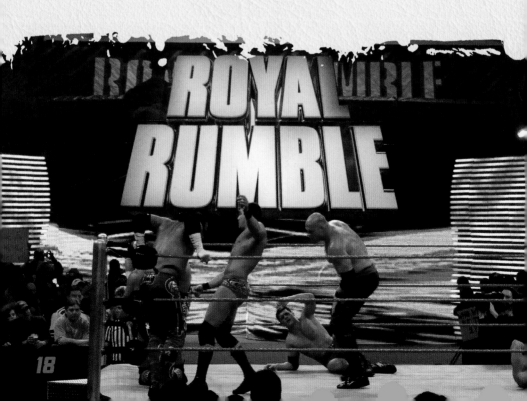

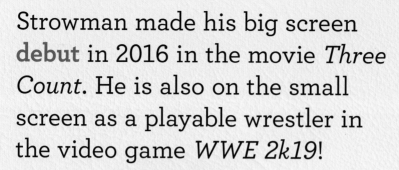

Strowman made his big screen **debut** in 2016 in the movie *Three Count.* He is also on the small screen as a playable wrestler in the video game *WWE 2k19!*

GLOSSARY

championship – a game, match, or race held to find a first-place winner.

debut – to appear for the first time.

match – a competition in which wrestlers fight against each other.

roster – a list of active wrestlers.

tag team – a division made up of teams of two people. Wrestlers tag their partner to get in and out of the match.

Wrestlemania – WWE's biggest event of the year.

ONLINE RESOURCES

Booklinks
NONFICTION NETWORK
FREE! ONLINE NONFICTION RESOURCES

To learn more about
Braun Strowman, please visit
abdobooklinks.com or scan
this QR code. These links
are routinely monitored and
updated to provide the most
current information available.

INDEX